P9-BYT-895

Maya Angelou

Phenomenal Woman

Paintings by *Paul Gauguin*

Edited by Linda Sunshine

A Welcome Book

Random House
NEW YORK

Pretty women wonder where my secret lies.

I'm not cute or built to suit

    a fashion model's size

        But when I start to tell them,

            They think I'm telling lies.

I say,
It's in the reach of my arms,
The span of my hips,
The stride of my step,
The curl of my lips.

I'm a woman
Phenomenally.
Phenomenal woman,
That's me.

I walk

into a room

Just as cool

as you please,

And to a man,
The fellows stand or
Fall down
on their knees.

Then they swarm
around me,
A hive of honey bees.

I say,
It's the fire in my eyes,
And the flash of my teeth,
The swing in my waist,
And the joy in my feet.

I'm a woman
Phenomenally.
Phenomenal woman,
That's me.

Men themselves
have wondered
What they see in me.

They try so much
But they can't touch
My inner mystery.

When I try
to show them,
They say
they still can't see.

I say,

It's in the arch of my back,

The sun of my smile,

The ride of my breasts,

The grace of my style.

I'm a woman

Phenomenally.

Phenomenal woman,

That's me.

Now you understand
Just why my head's
not bowed.

I don't shout
or jump about
Or have to talk
real loud.

When you see me passing,

It ought to make you proud.

I say,

It's in the click of my heels,

The bend of my hair,

The palm of my hand,

The need for my care.

'Cause I'm a woman
Phenomenally.
Phenomenal woman,
That's me.

Maya Angelou

"All of my work is meant to say, 'You may encounter many defeats but you must not be defeated.' In fact, the encountering may be the very experience which creates the vitality and the power to endure."

—As quoted in *The Norton Anthology of African American Literature*

She was born Marguerite Johnson on April 28, 1928, in St. Louis, Missouri, but her brother Bailey nicknamed her Maya ("mine"). Educated in Stamps, Arkansas, and San Francisco, California, she is a woman of rare talents and unprecedented accomplishments. Poet, writer, performer, teacher, and director, Maya Angelou is the author of the bestselling autobiographies *I Know Why the Caged Bird Sings* (nominated for a National Book Award), *Gather Together in My Name*, and *The Heart of a Woman*, as well as five collections of poetry and the poem "On the Pulse of Morning," which she read at the inauguration of President William Jefferson Clinton, the first African American and the first woman to be so honored. She has published two collections of essays and three children's books. She once said, "I write for the Black voice and for any ear which can hear it."

In theater, she produced, directed, and starred in *Cabaret for Freedom* in collaboration with Godfrey Cambridge at New York's Village Gate; starred in Genet's *The Blacks* at the St. Mark's Playhouse; and adapted Sophocles' *Ajax*, which premiered at the Mark Taper Forum in Los Angeles in 1974. She wrote the original screenplay for the film *Georgia, Georgia*, and wrote and produced *Black, Blues, Black*, a ten-part television series on African traditions in American life. She has acted in numerous documentaries, feature films such as *How to Make an American Quilt*, and television shows, including *Roots* and *Touched by an Angel*. She has received many honorary degrees, is on the board of trustees of the American Film Institute, and is also one of the few female members of the Directors Guild. Fluent in English, Italian, Spanish, French, Arabic, and West African Fanti, she lectures frequently and contributes to many magazines and periodicals. She is the Reynolds Professor at Wake Forest University, Winston-Salem, North Carolina.

In 1998, she made her directorial debut with Miramax's feature film *Down in the Delta*. For all these things and for the tender strength of her voice and vision, Maya Angelou is among the most respected and admired women in the world.

"Painting is the most beautiful of all the arts; in it all feelings are summed up. Looking at it each one can, through his imagination, create a novel; one single glance can engulf the soul in the most profound memories. . . ."
— From "Synthetic Notes," 1884–5

Paul Gauguin was born in Paris on June 7, 1848. At twenty, he joined the navy and sailed around the world. In 1873 he married a young Dutch girl named Mette Sophie Gad. "When we were married, I had no idea he was inclined to the arts," Mette later wrote in a letter to Jean de Rotochamp. The couple had five children and Gauguin worked as a stockbroker to support the family. For the next twelve years, his only escape from a respectable, bourgeois life was that he took up painting as a weekend hobby.

Becoming more serious about his art, he exhibited a painting in a group show in the early 1880s, and one reviewer, Joris-Karl Huysmans, wrote of his painting: "M. Gauguin is the first in years to have tried to represent the woman of our time." In 1883, Gauguin suddenly quit his job to paint full-time. Several years of family conflict followed until he finally abandoned his wife and children. In 1888, he joined his friend Vincent van Gogh in Arles where they planned to work together, but their conflicting temperaments soon created problems. One evening, van Gogh tried to attack Gauguin with a razor and wound up slicing off his own ear. Van Gogh was put in an asylum and Gauguin returned to Brittany.

Following a lifelong penchant for exotic places, Gauguin came to believe that his only salvation lay in abandoning modern civilization and Western culture for a purer, simpler way of life. "I am a great artist and I know it. It is because I am that I have endured such suffering," he wrote to his wife in March of 1892. "I have known for a long time what I am doing and why I do it. My artistic center is my brain and not elsewhere and I am strong because I am never sidetracked by others, and do what is in me."

He declared he wanted to live like a savage, and after trips to Panama and Martinique, he settled in Tahiti, where he painted brilliant canvases, freed from the limitations of impressionism and realism. According to some art scholars, modern art began with Paul Gauguin.

After years of illness, poverty, and suffering, the artist died on the island of Dominque in the Marquesas in 1903, at the age of 55.

Paul Gauguin

Compilation copyright © 2000 by Welcome Enterprises, Inc.
"Phenomenal Woman" copyright © 1978 by Maya Angelou

All rights reserved under International and Pan-American Copyright Conventions. Published in the United States by Random House, Inc., New York, and simultaneously in Canada by Random House of Canada Limited, Toronto.

RANDOM HOUSE and colophon are registered trademarks of Random House, Inc.

Random House website address: www.atrandom.com

Produced by Welcome Enterprises, Inc.
588 Broadway, New York, NY 10012

Edited by Linda Sunshine
A Greg/Clark Design

Library of Congress Cataloging-in-Publication Data

Angelou, Maya.
 Phenomenal woman / Maya Angelou ; paintings by Paul Gauguin ; edited by Linda Sunshine. — 1st ed.
  p.   cm.
 "A Welcome book."
  ISBN: 0-375-50406-0
  1. Women Poetry. I. Gauguin, Paul, 1848–1903. II. Sunshine, Linda. III. Title.
  PS3551.N464P48   2000
   811'.54--dc21   99-39134

Printed in Singapore by Tien Wah Press
9 8 7 6 5 4 3
First Edition

Illustration credits:

Front cover and page 7 (bottom): *Woman with a Fan*, 1902. Oil on canvas; 92 x 73 cm. Folkwang Museum, Essen, Germany. Giraudon/Art Resource, N.Y.

Page 3: *Portrait of Madeleine Bernard*. Musee de Peinture et de Sculpture, Grenoble, France. Erich Lessing/Art Resource, N.Y.

Page 4: *Woman of the Mango* (*Vahine no te Vi*), 1892. Oil on canvas; 72.7 x 44.5 cm. Baltimore Museum of Art: The Cone Collection, formed by Dr. Claribel Cone and Miss Etta Cone of Baltimore, Maryland. BMA 1950-213.

Pages 6–7: *Fatata te Miti* (*By the Sea*), 1892. Oil on canvas; 67.9 x 91.5 cm. Chester Dale Collection © 1999 Board of Trustees, National Gallery of Art, Washington.

Pages 8–9: *Why Are You Angry?* (*No Te Aha Oe Riri*), 1895–1896. Oil on canvas; 94.9 x 129.5 cm. Mr. and Mrs. Martin A. Ryerson Collection. 1933.1119. Photograph courtesy of The Art Institute of Chicago.

Pages 10–11: *Riders on the Beach*, 1902. Private collection.

Page 12: *Tahitian Girl* (painting sketch). Musee de Peinture et de Sculpture, Grenoble, France. Giraudon/Art Resource, N.Y.

Page 15 and 31: *Self Portrait with Idol*, 1893. San Antonio Museum of Art, San Antonio, Texas. Giraudon/Art Resource, N.Y.

Page 17 and back cover: *The King's Wife* (*Te arii vahine*), 1896. Oil on canvas; 97 x 130 cm. Pushkin Museum of Fine Arts, Moscow, Russia. Erich Lessing/Art Resource, N.Y.

Page 18: *Vairamuti*, 1897. Musee d'Orsay, Paris, France. Scala/Art Resource, N.Y.

Page 19: *Nude Woman among the Waves*, 1889. Cleveland Museum of Art, Cleveland, Ohio. Erich Lessing/Art Resource, N.Y.

Page 20–21: *Three Tahitians*, 1898. National Gallery of Scotland, Edinburgh.

Page 22: *Crouching Tahitian Woman*, Study for *Nafea Faaipoipo* (When Will you Marry?) [1892]. Pastel and charcoal over preliminary drawing in charcoal, selectively stumped, and squared with black chalk on wove paper; 1891/92. 55.5 x 48 cm. Gift of Tiffany and Margaret Blake. 1944.578 recto. Photograph courtesy of The Art Institute of Chicago.

Page 25: *Ea Haereia oe*. (Where are you going?), 1893. Hermitage, St. Petersburg, Russia. Scala/Art Resource, N.Y.

Page 26: *Tahitian Girls on the Beach*, 1892. Honolulu Academy of Arts, Honolulu, Hawaii. Giraudon/Art Resource, N.Y.

Page 27: *Birth of Tahitian Christ*. Hermitage, St. Petersburg, Russia. Scala/Art Resource, N.Y.

Page 28–29: *What, are you jealous? (Aha or feii?)*. Pushkin Museum of Fine Arts, Moscow, Russia. Scala/Art Resource, N.Y.

Page 30: photograph credit Steve Dunwell.